Quick Draw

Fairies and Princesses

KINGFISHER
BOSTON

How to use this book

1. Trace the grid opposite. You can use any size paper as long as the grid proportions are the same as the one in this book. The grid squares will help you position your drawing and ensure that the different stages are correctly scaled.

2. Use a light pencil line to draw. That way you can erase the lines much more easily.

3. Copy the shapes in Step 1 and then add the new shapes in Step 2 and so on. As you add each step, your picture will begin to take shape.

4. When you have copied each step, erase the extra lines from the earlier step—to eventually reveal the final shape (as shown in the last step).

5. Now color in your finished picture.

As you become more confident, you might find that you no longer need the grid squares. You might want to add your own finishing touches to the illustrations, such as background plants, to create a scene.

Dancing fairy

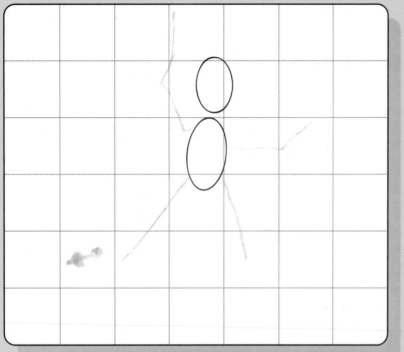

Step 1

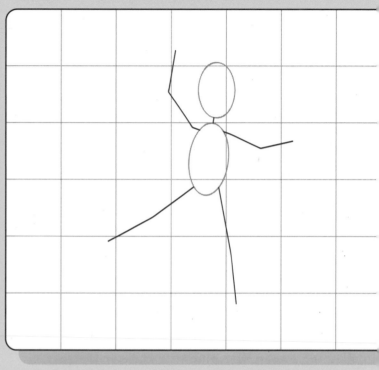

Step 2

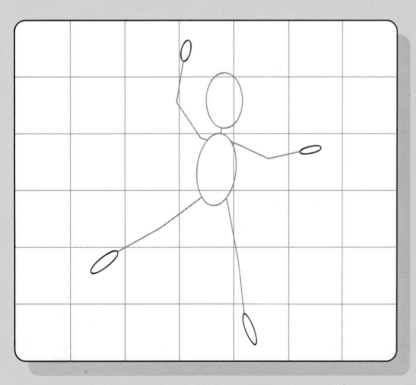

Step 3

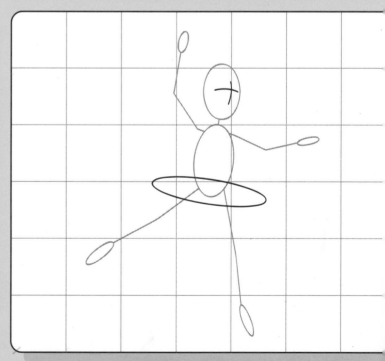

Step 4

Step 5

Step 6

tep 7

Step 8

Fairy-tale knight

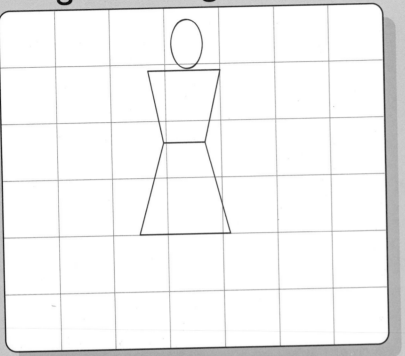

Step 1

Step 2

Step 3

Step 4

Step 5

Step 6

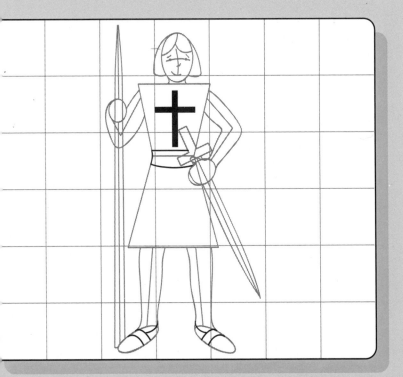

tep 7

Step 8

Fairy-tale princess

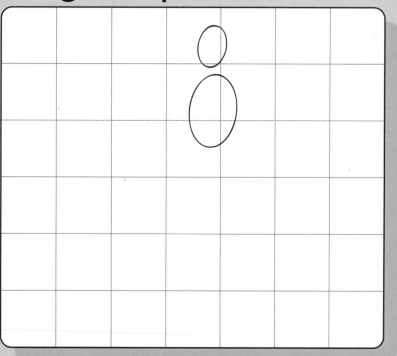

Step 1

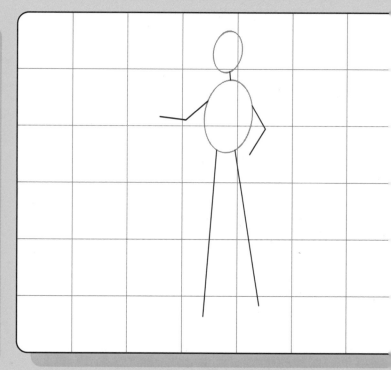

Step 2

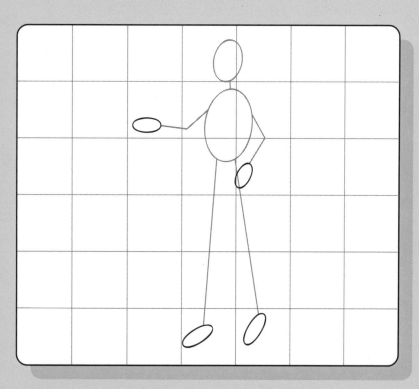

Step 3

Step 4

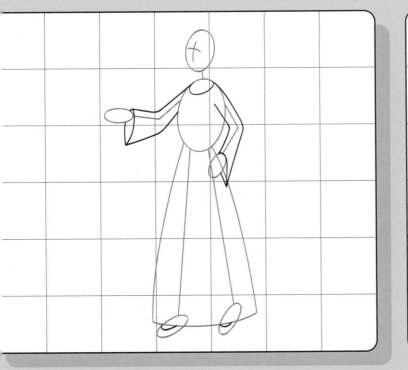

tep **5**

Step **6**

tep **7**

Step **8**

Fairy-tale prince

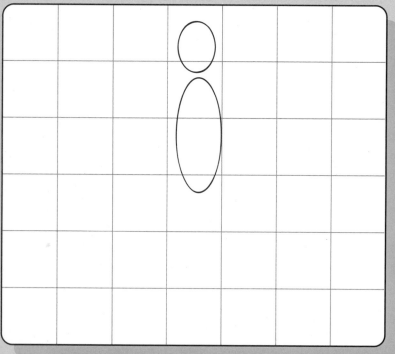

Step 1

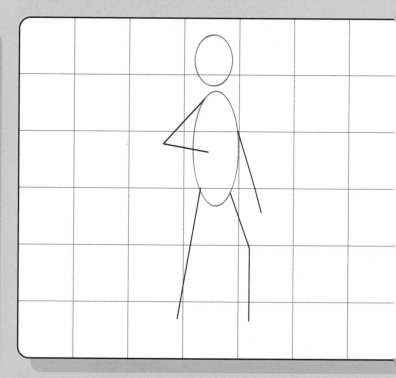

Step 2

Step 3

Step 4

Step 5

Step 6

Step 7

Step 8

Fairy-tale queen

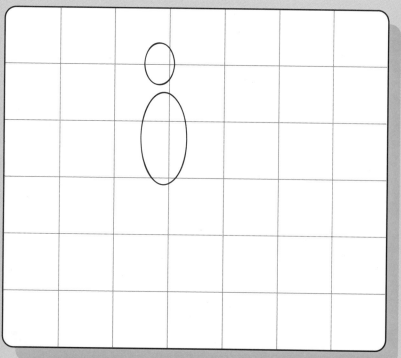

Step 1

Step 2

Step 3

Step 4

tep 5

tep 7

Step 8

Fairy-tale king

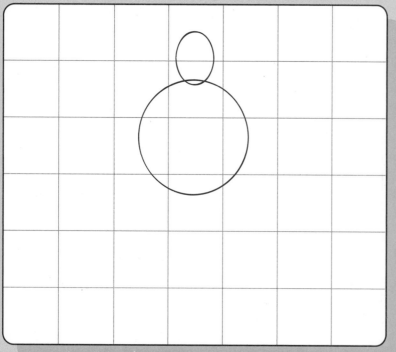

Step 1

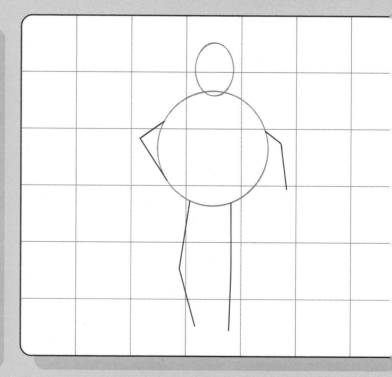

Step 2

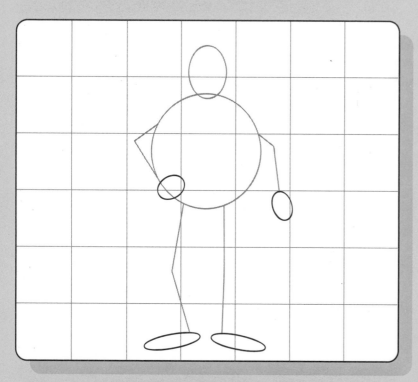

Step 3

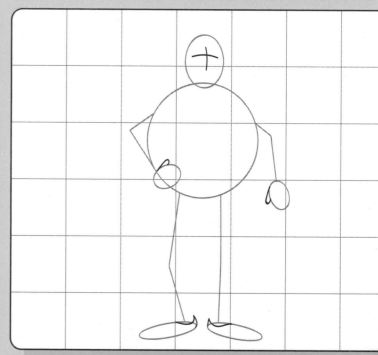

Step 4

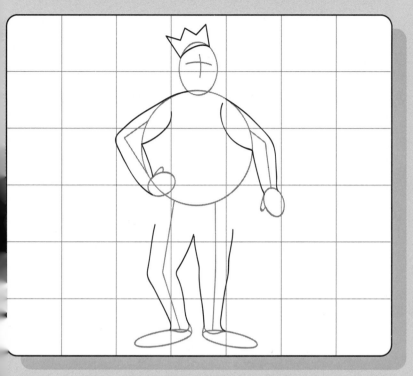

Step 5

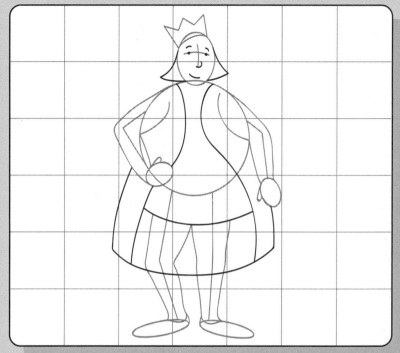

Step 6

Step 7

Step 8

Cinderella before the ball

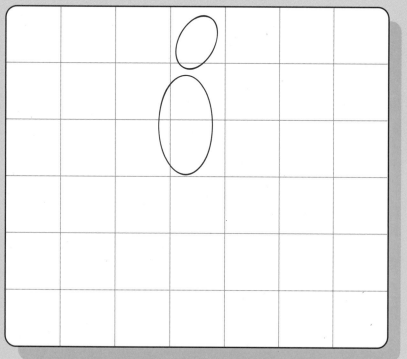

Step 1

Step 2

Step 3

Step 4

Step 5

Step 6

Step 7

Step 8

Fairy godmother

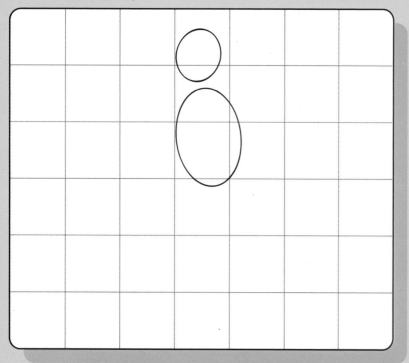

Step 1

Step 2

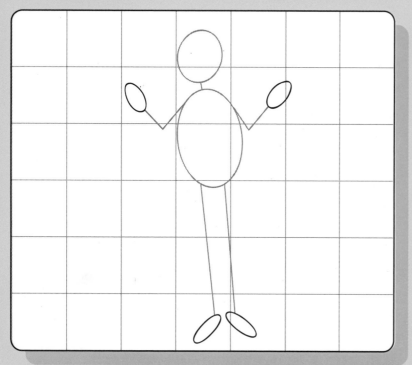

Step 3

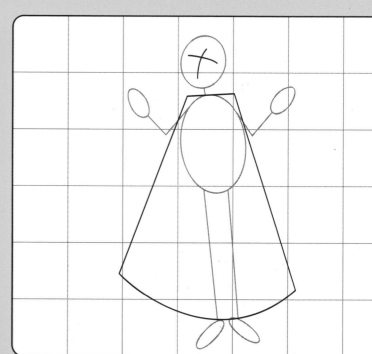

Step 4

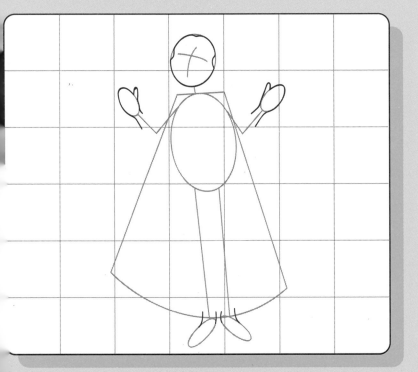

Step 5

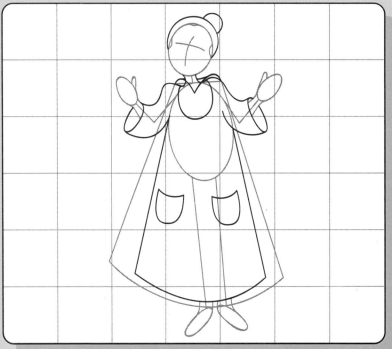

Step 6

Step 7

Step 8

Princess wearing a ball gown

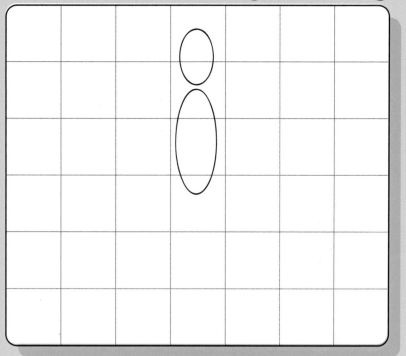

Step 1

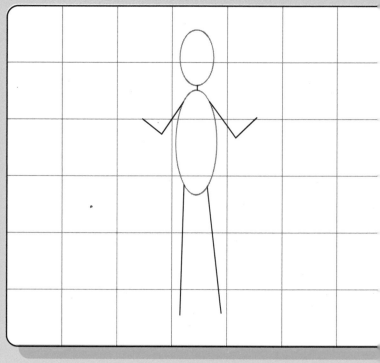

Step 2

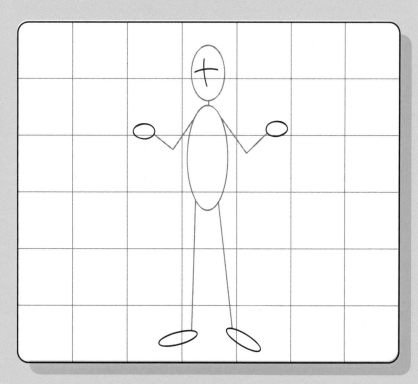

Step 3

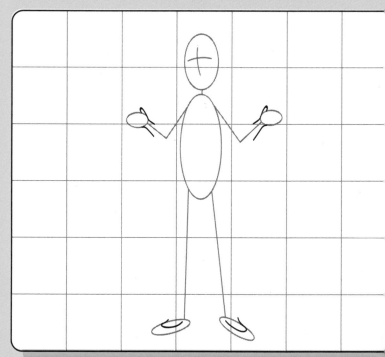

Step 4

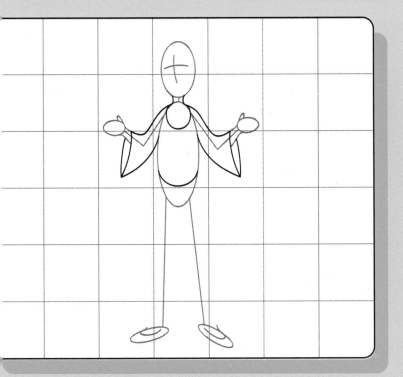

tep 5

Step 6

tep 7

Step 8

Pixie

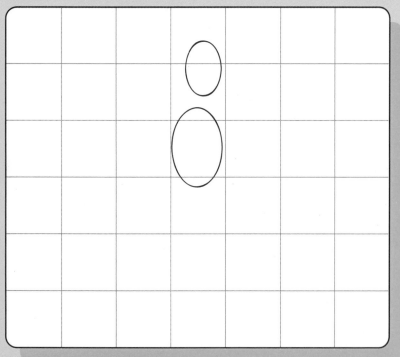

Step 1

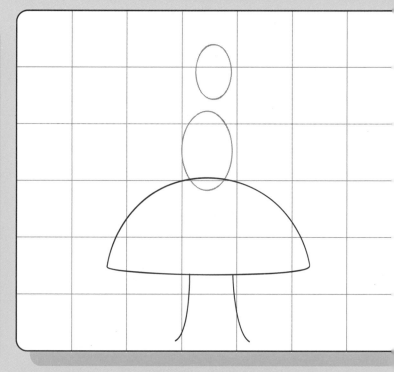

Step 2

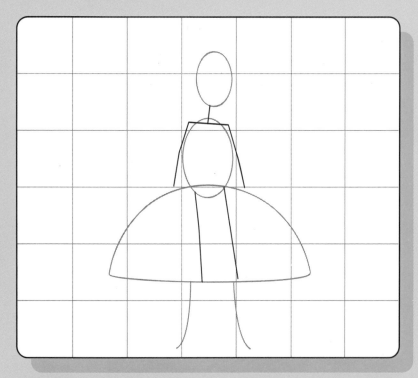

Step 3

Step 4

Step 5

Step 6

Step 7

Step 8

Mermaid

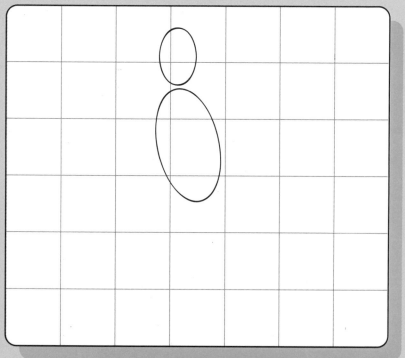

Step 1

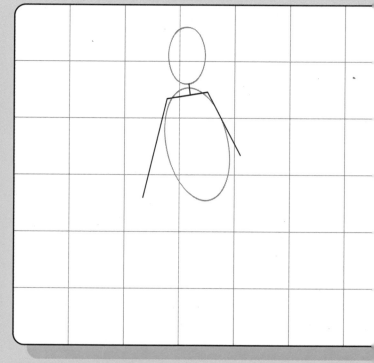

Step 2

Step 3

Step 4

Step 5

Step 6

tep 7

Step 8

Baby fairy

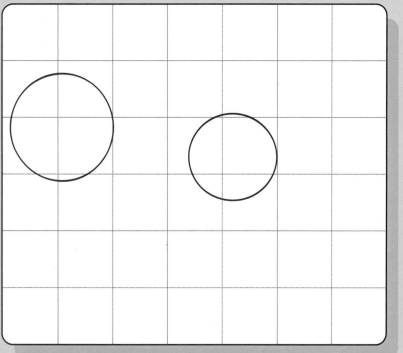

Step 1

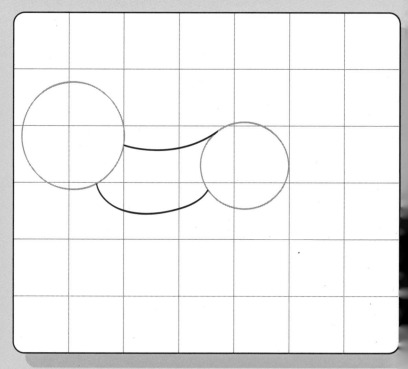

Step 2

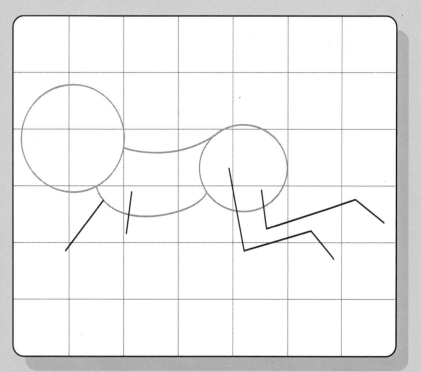

Step 3

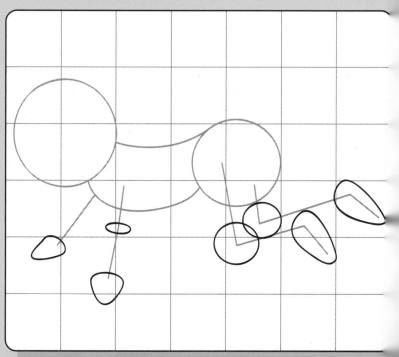

Step 4

Step 5

Step 6

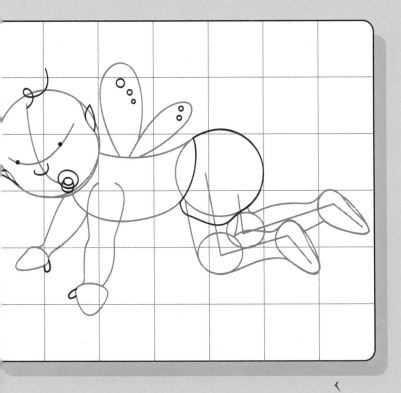

Step 7

Step 8

Tooth fairy

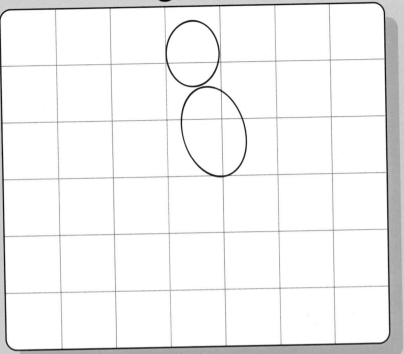

Step 1

Step 2

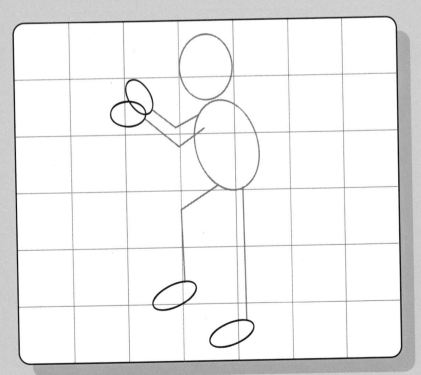

Step 3

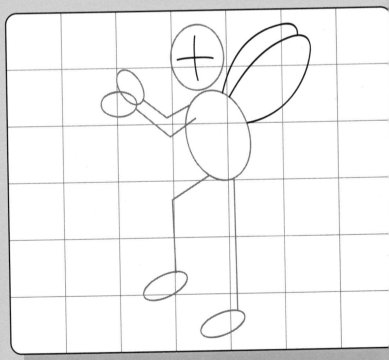

Step 4

Step 5

Step 6

tep 7

Step 8

Wild-strawberry fairy

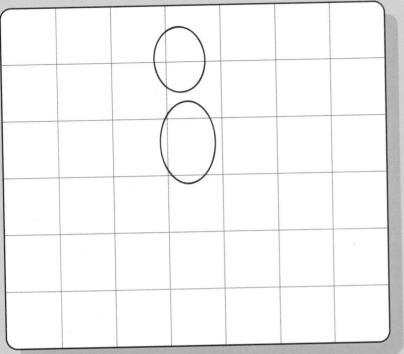

Step 1

Step 2

Step 3

Step 4

Step 5

Step 6

tep 7

Step 8

KINGFISHER
a Houghton Mifflin Company imprint
222 Berkeley Street
Boston, Massachusetts 02116
www.houghtonmifflinbooks.com

First published in 2008
10 9 8 7 6 5 4 3 2 1

1TR/1107/THOM/IGS(SCHOY)/120BLT/C

Produced for Kingfisher by The Peter Bull Art Studio

For Kingfisher:
Associate creative director: Mike Davis
Designers: Ray Bryant and Emy Manby
Senior production controller: Jessamy Oldfield
DTP manager: Nicky Studdart

LIBRARY OF CONGRESS CATALOGING-IN-PUBLICATION DATA
Quick draw: fairies & princesses.—1st ed.
    p. cm.
 ISBN 978-0-7534-6201-0
 1. Fairies in art—Juvenile literature. 2. Princesses in art—
Juvenile literature. 3. Drawing—Technique—Juvenile
literature.
 NC825.F22Q85 2008
 743'.87—dc22
                                2007031945

 ISBN 978-0-7534-6201-0

 Printed in India